MW01612257

What's in the Bible About Life Together?

What's in the Bible,
and Why Should I Care?

What's in the Bible About

Life Together?

Paul E. Stroble

ABINGDON PRESS
NASHVILLE

WHAT'S IN THE BIBLE ABOUT LIFE TOGETHER?
by Paul E. Stroble

Copyright © 2008 by Abingdon Press

All rights reserved. No part of this work may be reproduced or transmitted in any form or by any means, electronic or mechanical, including photocopying and recording, or by any information or retrieval system, except as may be expressly permitted in the 1976 Copyright Act or in writing from the publisher. Requests for permission should be addressed in writing to Permissions Office, P. O. Box 801, 201 Eighth Avenue, South, Nashville, Tennessee 37202-0801, or call (615) 749-6421.

Scripture quotations in this publication, unless otherwise indicated, are from the New Revised Standard Version of the Bible, copyright © 1989 by the Division of Christian Education of the National Council of the Churches of Christ in the United States of America, and are used by permission. All rights reserved.

 Abingdon Press

ISBN-13: 978-0-687-65304-1

Manufactured in the United States of America

08 09 10 11 12 13 14 15 16 17—10 9 8 7 6 5 4 3 2 1

CONTENTS

Paul Stroble is an elder of the Illinois Great Rivers Conference of The United Methodist Church. He studied at Greenville College, Yale Divinity School, and the University of Virginia. He has served as a parish pastor and volunteer leader at several churches and as a college teacher and seminary instructor. He currently teaches in the history department and Honors College at the University of Akron, where he earned an Excellence in Teaching Award. Paul is a writer-researcher for the United Methodist curriculum *FaithLink* and has written numerous articles, essays, poems, and curricular materials. Among his several books are *Paul and Galatians, What Do Other Faiths Believe?* and *What About Religion and Science? A Study of Reason and Faith*, all for Abingdon Press, and *You Gave Me a Wide Place: Holy Places of Our Lives*, published by Upper Room Books. Paul has also written two books about his hometown, Vandalia, Illinois, and contributes to local historical efforts. Paul enjoys drawing, shopping in antique stores, and spending time with his wife, Dr. Beth Stroble, and their daughter, Emily.

About This Bible Study Series

Have you ever wondered what the Bible is all about? What's in it? Why is it so important for Christians? Is it relevant for people in the 21st century? Should I care about what's in the Bible? Why? What difference will it make in my life? The study series *What's in the Bible, and Why Should I Care?* offers opportunities for you to explore these questions and others by opening the Bible, reading it, prayerfully reflecting on what the Bible readings say, and making connections between the readings and your daily life. The series title points to the two essential features of meaningful Bible study: reading the Bible and applying it to your life. This unique and exciting Bible study series is designed to help you accomplish this two-fold purpose.

The books in *What's in the Bible, and Why Should I Care?* are designed to help you find relevance, hope, and meaning for your life even if you have little or no experience with the Bible. You will discover ways the Bible can help you with major questions you may have about the nature of God, how God relates to us, and how we can relate to God. Such questions continue to be relevant whether you are new to church life, a long-time member of church, or a seeker who is curious and wants to know more.

Whether you read a study book from this series on your own or with others in a Bible study group, you will experience benefits. You will gain confidence in reading the Bible as you learn how to use and study it. You will find meaning and hope in the people and teachings of the Bible. More importantly, you will discover more about who God is and how God relates to you personally through the Bible.

What's in the Bible?

Obviously, we answer the question "What's in the Bible?" by reading it. As Christians, we understand that the stories of our faith come to us through this holy book. We view the Bible as the central document for all we believe and profess about God. It contains stories about those who came before us in the Christian faith, but it is more than a book of stories about them. The Bible tells us about God. It tells how a particular group of people in a particular part of the world over an extended period of time, inspired by God, understood and wrote about who God is and how God acted among them. The Bible also tells what God expected from them. Its value and meaning reach to all people across all time—past, present, and future.

Why Should I Care?

Meaningful Bible study inspires people to live their lives according to God's will and way. As you read through the stories collected in the Bible, you will see again and again a just and merciful God who creates, loves, saves, and heals. You will see that God expects people, who are created in the image of God (Genesis 1), to live their lives as just and merciful people of God. You will discover that God empowers people to live according to God's way. You will learn that in spite of our sin, of our tendency to turn away from God and God's ways, God continues to love and save us. This theme emerges from and unifies all the books that have been brought together in the Holy Bible.

Christians believe that God's work of love and salvation finds confirmation and completion through the life, ministry, death, and resurrection of Jesus Christ. We accept God's free gift of love and salvation through Jesus Christ; and out of gratitude, we commit our lives to following him and living as he taught us to live. Empowered by God's Holy Spirit, we grow in faith, service, and love toward God and neighbor. I pray that this Bible study series will help you experience God's love and power in your daily life. I pray that it will help you grow in your faith and commitment to Jesus Christ.

Pamela Dilmore

When I was in my early twenties, I served two country congregations as a supply preacher over a summer. Each Sunday, I preached at the first church, all the while keeping my eye on the clock so I could chat with members of the congregation after the service *and* have time for the three- or four-mile trip on state and county roads to the second church. Once there, I'd also make time to chat and visit the worshipers.

One morning, a young woman at the second church asked me to pray for her because she was seeking God's will in a personal matter. Eager to be helpful, I promised to pray for her and to preach on that topic. The following Sunday, she wasn't at church; and I don't remember what I preached, but I probably talked about Scripture reading, friends' advice, and other ways in which we can learn to know God's will in our daily decisions. I may have talked about how our lives are never perfect or free of trouble but that God works for good in our circumstances (Romans 8:28). I may have also talked about the importance of being "in touch" with God through daily prayer so that we might be sensitive to his presence.

Many of us tend to think of "seeking God's will" as a matter of guidance when we have to make difficult choices. That's a proper way to think about God's will; but over the years, I've realized that the Bible is uncomfortably clear about another aspect of God's will: God wants us to be loving and holy. This is God's will for all Christians, regardless of our choices and circumstances; it's not negotiable!

What is love? There are different words for love in the Greek language, the original language of most of the New Testament. These "loves" are different but complementary, *Philia* means "the love of friendship" and "common interest"; and *eros* is "intimate, romantic love." *Agape* means the kind of "unconditional, voluntary love" that we find in certain Scriptures, for example, the well-known 1 Corinthians 13:1-8 emphasizes *agape* as more important than self-displaying moral, religious, and doctrinal achievement. In that passage, *agape* defines our very lives in so far as we are committed to and work for the benefit of one another rather than in terms of personal achievement.)

In John's Gospel, the *agape* that we show as Christians reflects the love that exists between the Son of God and God the Father. As Jesus did the will of his Father and gave up his life for our salvation (John 15:12-13), so we, in a far more imperfect way, love one another.

What is holiness? We think of a holy person as someone whose sanctity and sacrifice lie far beyond our own modest efforts. Alternately, a holy person is one who acts better than others, an embodiment of the expression *holier than thou*. However, the Old Testament contains over 830 references to holiness (or to related terms); and aspects of holiness appear nearly 230 times in the New Testament.[1] So the Bible itself considers holiness something positive.

As God is holy, so he calls those who love him to be holy, too (Leviticus 19:1-2). Followers of Jesus are called "holy" over 60 times in the New Testament.[2] Paul closely linked love and holiness. In 1 Corinthians 6:11, he tells the church that "you were washed, you were sanctified [made holy], you were justified in the name of the Lord Jesus Christ and in the Spirit of our God." However, the church was not being loving. They had lawsuits, immorality, factions, and members aggrandizing themselves. Paul reminded them that they were already holy people, gifted with ministries of the Spirit (1 Corinthians 12). Yet they lacked important love for one another.

Paul taught that our holiness shows itself through the "ministry of reconciliation" (2 Corinthians 5:18), where we are "ambassadors for Christ, since God is making his appeal through us" (2 Corinthians 5:20). We prove God exists according to how well we love one another. We might disprove God exists according to how well we love one another. We might disprove many skeptics' arguments if we served and loved others in a powerful way.

People attend church for different motives: It's the right thing to do, we enjoy the worship, we like to serve, we learn about the Bible.

We may have lesser motives: We make social contacts we can use else-where, we like having a place we can "run things," we feel like we have to go to church. Paul said God gives us the Holy Spirit "to equip the saints [people blessed with God's holiness] for the work of ministry, for building up the body of Christ" (Ephesians 4:12). Being a Christian means accepting the loving responsibility to help others also grow in Christ. In fact, that's why God blesses us with his grace: to help and affirm one another and to grow in our life together. That's one of the best reasons to attend church.

In these sessions, we'll look at aspects of our life together as Christians. We'll think about ways that we grow as Christians in our inner selves. We'll also think about how God's moral laws define our relationships with one another. We'll examine Jesus' teachings about forgiveness, service, and fellowship. We'll look at God's special love for the needy of the world and the ways God calls us to reflect God's own love in our relationships and attitudes. Ideally, there's no such thing as a Christian who has to "go it alone."

I hope that woman, nearly 30 years ago, discovered God's will for her decision. Meanwhile, I praise God for all his help and blessings to me over the years, blessings that include friends and congregations I have known, blessings more than I could have asked or imagined (Ephesians 3:20-21). Let us turn to Scriptures that will help us realize God's will and purposes in our life together.

Paul E. Stroble

---

[1]From *Baker Theological Dictionary of the Bible,* by Walter A. Elwell, editor (Baker Books, 1996); pages 342-43.
[2]From *Baker Theological Dictionary of the Bible;* page 343.

Chapter One

The Law Reveals
God's Way of Life

Bible Readings
Exodus 20:2-17; Leviticus 19:17-18; Deuteronomy 5:6-21; 6:4-13; 10:12-22

The Questions
We all live by laws, rules, and expectations. What does God expect from us? How are God's laws related to God's love? How do God's laws help us love one another?

_____

_____

_____

_____

_____

_____

_____

_____

_____

_____

_____

_____

_____

Psalm

> How sweet are your words to my taste,
>
> > sweeter than honey to my mouth!
>
> Through your precepts I get understanding;
>
> > therefore I hate every false way.
>
> Your word is a lamp to my feet
>
> > and a light to my path.
>
> Psalm 119:103, 105

A Prayer

Lord, your laws are wonderful and give us understanding. Guide us like a light so we may grow in love and wisdom; in Christ we pray. Amen.

Spiritual Growth and Life Together

How is your self-image as a Christian? When I was young, I felt close to God while praying, reading the Bible, and thinking about my morning devotions; but my faith didn't seem strong and confident when I was out in the world with exasperating people, everyday conflicts, careless drivers, my own self-doubts, and a variety of challenges. I felt quite inadequate by day's end. I thought, *Maybe I'm not even saved!*

I had two misconceptions. First, I didn't realize I needed time to grow. God doesn't tap us on the head and make us into mature Christians for the rest of our lives, though people might expect that from us. Our faith typically grows as we meet our daily responsibilities, fail in our faith, try again, grow, and experience God's help over the "long haul." My other misconception was that I could grow as a Christian more or less privately. That old hymn "In the Garden" is one of my favorites; but our faith is never *only* a private, comforting relationship with Jesus, because he calls us to reach out to others in a Jesus-like way (1 John 3:14-16).

Our love for one another is itself a gift from God; but even divinely supplied love isn't easy, for we encounter unlovable people, we're tempted by circumstances, and we encounter problems that don't have simple solutions. The more seriously we pursue spiritual growth, the more we discover our own need for God's grace, healing, and guidance. We also discover that our life with others changes. God's laws are all about guiding our individual and communal spiritual growth, that is, our relationship with God and our relationship with others.

How do you perceive your own spiritual growth?
(1) Pretty good at the moment
(2) One step forward and two steps back
(3) Better some days than others
(4) What spiritual growth?

REFLECT

Love the Lord
Deuteronomy 6:4-13

Deuteronomy 6 contains the heartbeat of Judeo-Christian faith: placing one's trust and love in God. It calls us to complete allegiance to God in every aspect of our lives. Several years ago I visited a rabbi at his synagogue. Although my Hebrew is rusty, I recognized the Hebrew words above the ark portion of the sanctuary: Verse 4, which is translated, "Hear, O Israel: The LORD is our God, the LORD alone" (New Revised Standard Version) or "The LORD our God, the LORD is one"[1] (New International Version) or "The LORD our God is one LORD" (King James Version). This statement is known as the *Shema*, the Hebrew word for "hear" or "listen" that begins this verse.

Since Hebrew has no verb (other than the imperative *listen*), the words can be understood in different though complementary ways. The statement affirms God's oneness: "The Lord our God is one Lord and not several gods." The statement could be emphatic: "The Lord, and only the Lord, is our God." It could be a statement of praise: "The Lord our God is an incomparable and unique Lord." The statement also implies no separation between one's everyday life and one's religion: "The Lord our God is Lord over the whole of our lives."

The phrase "the Lord our God" does not mean that Israel (or anyone) can control and possess God or use God in order to gain status. Mistreating others and advancing ourselves in the name of God are always wrong. If I can paraphrase the pronoun *our*, it would be: God is "our God" because God adopted us through God's own choice, love, and initiative. We have a wonderful responsibility to help one another learn, grow in religious devotion, and serve together.

What's in the Bible?
Read Deuteronomy 6:4-13. What challenges you about God's commands? Does God seem loving or demanding or both? How do you respond to the command to love and serve God alone?

Verse 5 says, "You shall love the LORD your God with all your heart, and with all your soul, and with all your might." How do we love God? The Bible speaks clearly to showing love through our actions: through acts of worship and through acts of mercy, justice, and kindness toward one another. This instruction seems simple on the surface; but if we think a little more deeply, we can see that it contains challenges.

Expressing our love for God is not always easy. We may have to deal with things in our lives that make loving God difficult. Perhaps our father or mother (or both) fell short, and we aren't sure how to relate to God as a loving parent. Perhaps a tragedy causes us to feel bitter toward God. My grandmother died in a fire when I was young, and I didn't realize how much anger I harbored toward God until years later. Those were years, I should add, when God was doing wonderful things in my life in spite of my buried bitterness.

When you read the Psalms, you will discover all kinds of emotional feelings directed toward God, including disappointment in God's apparent absence or slowness to respond. Such feelings often affect our motivation or ability to act in loving ways, yet these psalms assure us that God's love is steadfast in spite of our feelings.

What experiences have helped you draw closer to God or made you feel more distant from God? What do you think about honestly expressing to God feelings such as anger, bitterness, or disappointment?

REFLECT

God also calls us to grow our faith by living and teaching our religious traditions and by passing our faith to others (verses 7-9). I had a friend who said she was not instructing her young son in religion because she wanted him to discover faith for himself. She was half-right; children cherish things best when they decide for themselves. I was raised in church and yet didn't embrace an active faith until I went to college and made my own decisions. However, my friend was missing an important opportunity to introduce her son to religion and thus lay a foundation for him that would be meaningful later on (verse 7). As Christians, we have inherited our faith from those who came before us; and we are called to pass that faith to those who come after us.

What was your childhood experience with religion, if any? Did your experience hinder or help your adult efforts at faith? Who has been an important teacher or model for you in your life of faith?

R E F L E C T

God doesn't wait until we're sufficiently spiritual to relate to us and to help us. God helps us love through our prayers, our Bible reading, through worship, through other people, and through our life experiences of God's help and faithfulness. God also helps us when we fall short. In this session, God calls the Israelites to recall the amazing things God did for them, even as they grumbled and were disobedient (verses 10-12). While we may be inconsistent in our expressions of our love for God, God's love is steadfast. We can count on God's love to be there for us, to empower us, and to restore us even when we fail in our own expressions of love.

The Ten Commandments
Exodus 20:2-17; Deuteronomy 5:6-21

When I was little, religion seemed all about rules: Don't play cards, drink, swear, or mow your lawn on Sunday. I later learned that being a Christian is *not* about rules and performance. Nor is being a Christian primarily about virtue and character. A Christian is one who has accepted the free gift of God's grace through Christ. A Christian relies upon God's power and not upon his or her own goodness. I stress this before we read the Ten Commandments because we're apt to put the cart before the horse and believe that we earn our salvation through keeping the commandments. Actually we keep the commandments out of love as a response to God's love; never, ever do we keep them as a way to earn God's love. The Ten Commandments are a gift from God that guides us in our life together as God's people.

What's in the Bible?
Read the Ten Commandments in Exodus 20:2-17 and Deuteronomy 5:6-21. How are these readings similar? How are they different? Do some commandments seem more difficult to keep than others? Which ones? Why? What do they say to you about life together as God's people?

The Ten Commandments are also known as the Decalogue, meaning "ten words" or "ten statements." They are timeless ethical principles; but even more, they're a crucial part of God's covenant with his people and guide our great responsibility toward God and one another.

In Exodus 19, God offers a covenant (agreement) to the people of Israel; and the Ten Commandments specify the obligations of the people who would choose to enter into the covenant with God. They brought the Israelites, a disparate people, together by defining ways to love God and one another. The first four—have no other gods besides the Lord, do not worship God through an idol, do not misuse the Lord's name, and keep the sabbath holy—have to do with our relationship with God. The remaining six—honor your parents, do not kill (the Hebrew word means "murder"), do not commit adultery, do not steal, do not lie or testify falsely about others, and do not desire what someone else has—have to do with our social relationships. Obedience to the laws reveals our identity as God's people and assures healthy relationship to God and to one another.

Bible Facts
Notice the similarity and difference between the Exodus and Deuteronomy versions of the sabbath commandment. Both recall and celebrate the Creation narrative in Genesis 1. Deuteronomy 5:14-15 adds a focus on the responsibility for social justice by recalling the Exodus.

Love Your Neighbor
Leviticus 19:17-18, 33-34

We've looked at the Ten Commandments; but did you know about the two commandments that, according to Jesus himself, are the greatest of all? (Mark 12:31). We read one of them earlier, Deuteronomy 6:5, which calls for love of God. Jesus also emphasized a second great commandment, our next Scripture reading, Leviticus 19:17-18.

What's in the Bible?
Read Leviticus 19:17-18, 33-34. How does this Bible reading speak to you? What thoughts or feelings do you have about loving your neighbor as yourself? about loving the alien?

"Who Do You Love?" is the title of a classic Bo Diddley song, but it's also a classic religious question. As we'll continue to see in these sessions, the Old Testament and Jesus challenge us to love fully and completely. In my opinion, the ending of Leviticus 19:18 is one of the most beautiful verses in the Bible: "You shall love your neighbor as yourself: I am the LORD." In verse 34, God instructs, "The alien who resides with you shall be to you as the citizen among you; you shall love the alien as yourself, for you were aliens in the land of Egypt: I am the LORD your God" (verse 34).

In Leviticus, *neighbor* implies fellow Israelites; but as we see from verse 34, the love God instructs also extends to non-Israelites. When I was in Sunday school as a child, I remember learning the answer to the question "Who is my neighbor?" The answer: everyone! How do we show love to everyone? It can be challenging to love people whose choices we dislike, whose lifestyles we disapprove of, those who are "out to get us" at our workplace, or who just annoy us. When we encounter people whose race, culture, or religion is different from our own, the challenge to love them increases. God, who created and loves all people, calls us and empowers us to love one another.

How do you answer the question "Who do you love?" Who is easy to love? Who is difficult or impossible to love? Why? Your answer might include specific individuals or types or groups of people.

REFLECT

Christian love can come across hypocritically if we say we love someone but do not express that love in our actions. Notice that the Ten Commandments and the two great commandments in Deuteronomy 6 and Leviticus 19 go together. We love God with our whole selves, and one way we love God is to love one another. However, love isn't just a favorable disposition or an emotion. People can sincerely say they love you yet treat you shabbily. Love for one another is an active process of refraining from behaviors that harm others and actively seeking the other person's benefit.

Why do you think actions might be a better indicator of love than feelings?

R E F L E C T

As I wrote earlier, God helps us grow in love for God; and God also helps us grow in love for one another. I have a friend who says, only half joking, that when she prays for patience, she hits all the red lights on the road. We can pray for love, and God may very well introduce annoying persons into our lives. The scary thing is that we do show people how much we love God by the way we love other people. It is good to know that God gives us the capacity to grow in love of neighbor.

As a private prayer exercise, write on a separate sheet of paper the names of people toward whom you don't feel much, if any, love. Go down the list, and talk to God about your feelings concerning each person: why you find them difficult to love, what happened, and so on. Be truthful to God. Then give your feelings to God, and ask God to help you concerning these people. Destroy your list to symbolize your trust that God hears your prayers.

R E F L E C T

God's Will
Deuteronomy 10:12-22

When we're serious about following God in our lives, God's will is an unavoidable issue; but knowing God's will can be difficult.

What's in the Bible?
Read Deuteronomy 10:12-22. What connections do you make between this Bible reading and the will of God? What does it say to you about God's will for our life together?

God wants us to walk God's way of love. Walking is a metaphor for life. We speak of "walking the straight and narrow" and those who "get off track." In the religious life, walking with God is living according to God's will and guidance. If we live only by God's moral code, we haven't gone quite far enough because God also wants a loving relationship with us. We walk with God by seeking to live our lives according to God's will. Deuteronomy 10:12 asks, "What does the LORD your God require of you?" and the answer quickly follows:

- to fear God
- to walk in God's ways
- to love God
- to serve God with the whole heart and soul
- to keep God's commandments and decrees

All around, an excellent model for how to live!

Two aspects of walking are its slowness compared to driving a car and the ability to be attentive to surroundings. How do these aspects make walking a great metaphor for our religious life?

REFLECT

Bible Facts
What does it mean to fear God? The Hebrew word used in Deuteronomy 10:12 means more than simply being afraid. It means respect and awe.

BIBLE FACTS

Although we're called to fear God, we shouldn't view God as some kind of unstable parent or demanding authority. God gives us the Bible so we can have plenty of assurance and assistance in understanding God's love and following God's will. Deuteronomy 10 reminds us that God is the Lord of all creation, who declares love for the people. God is just and merciful, especially to those who are most vulnerable: widows, orphans, and strangers. God provides. God keeps promises. God's people are called to be just and merciful in the same way that God is just and merciful.

Here's Why I Care
What insights have you gained from this chapter? What new things have you learned about God? about love? What can you do this week in order to live according to God's commandments?

A Prayer

God, your laws light our pathways and give us understanding. We thank you that you help us understand your love and the importance of love for one another. Help us perceive your presence in our lives, and help us grow; in Christ we pray. Amen.

---

[1]Scripture taken from the Holy Bible, NEW INTERNATIONAL VERSION®. Copyright ©1973, 1978, 1984 by International Bible Society. All rights reserved throughout the world. Used by permission of International Bible Society.

Chapter Two

The Prophets
Challenge Us to Return to God's Way

Bible Readings
Isaiah 33:15-16; Jeremiah 31:31-34; Amos 5:21-24; Micah 6:6-8

The Questions
What is God's way? How do we know when we are straying from God's way? How can the prophets help us return to God's way?

_____

_____

_____

_____

_____

_____

_____

_____

_____

_____

_____

_____

A Psalm

Create in me a clean heart, O God,

   and put a new and right spirit within me.

Do not cast me away from your presence,

   and do not take your holy spirit from me.

Restore to me the joy of your salvation,

   and sustain in me a willing spirit.

                                        Psalm 51:10-12

A Prayer

Lord, you give us your love and laws; but we're prone to stray from your will. Help us listen to what the prophets can teach us about your way of life. Renew your Spirit within us, and guide us in your wisdom; in Christ we pray. Amen.

Back to God

When I was ten years old, our vacation Bible school took a morning field trip to the nearest synagogue, which was several miles away in Centralia, Illinois. I don't remember much about the visit other than a positive feeling about the experience that led, years later, to my love and appreciation of the Jewish heritage of Christian faith. The prophets, who persistently called the people of Israel to return to God, are a key piece of this heritage.

North of my Illinois hometown, along US 51, a wooden cross once stood in the grass beside Bear Creek. The phrase "Get Right With God" was printed on the cross. Crosses such as this one, which was removed decades ago, were once a common sight that "preached" along American highways. I would paraphrase that message to say, "Through Jesus Christ, God already loves us dearly and has already done everything needed for us to get right with him. Now we need to learn about God's great work in Christ and have a close relationship with God and with one another." Obviously my paraphrase isn't as straightforward as the original!

God doesn't withhold his love until we step up; rather, God loved us enough to have given us the Law, the prophets, and Jesus. We are prone to wander, however. Sometimes we don't quite understand the responsibilities of our faith, and sometimes we just get discouraged. Sometimes we wander from God when we think we're quite spiritual and OK. In those times, we perform the various tasks of worship; but somehow our heart isn't focused on God, and our hearts lack love for others. Our love for God and for one another is the mark of a healthy relationship with God. The prophets can speak to us just as they spoke to the people of Israel. They call us to "get right with God."

How do you respond to the phrase Get right with God*? Have you ever thought you needed to get right with God? What was it like? How was God there for you?*

REFLECT

Rewards of the Righteous
Isaiah 33:15-16

The Hebrew prophets preached to and taught God's people during difficult times. The Israelites were ruled by a series of bad kings and strayed from God's will. The prophets called the people and the kings to repentance. If the people returned to God's will, at least some of the threats from neighboring nations might be forestalled.

What's in the Bible?
Read Isaiah 33:15-16. What challenges you in this reading? What does the Scripture reading say to you about what God wants? What connections do you make between this Scripture and contemporary life?

Isaiah lived during the 700's B.C. His prophecies are frequently quoted and alluded to in the New Testament. Isaiah 33 deals with the period of around 705-701 B.C. when the Judeans (the Southern Kingdom) revolted against Assyria. Jerusalem was attacked by the Assyrians. Jerusalem survived but not forever, for the Babylonians destroyed the city and the Temple in 586 B.C. By this time, the Northern Kingdom had fallen; and of course the Judeans did not want a similar fate.

Isaiah 33 concludes the section with words of hope. A confusing chapter with abrupt shifts, it begins with a condemnation of an enemy, possibly Assyria (verse 1), then turns into a prayer to God for safety and help (verses 3-4). Next, the passage contains expressions of confidence in God (verses 5-6), a description of social disorder (verses 7-9), and a promise from God himself (verses 10-13). In verse 14, the people ask who can live "with the devouring fire . . . with everlasting flames?"

An important question! It asks who can survive the presence of God, which is expressed in the image of fire. Verses 15-16 give the answer. God will favor those who walk righteously, speak uprightly, hate the profit that comes from oppression, reject bribes, won't listen to plots of murder, and won't look upon evil. Not only will such people survive the fire of God, but they will be rewarded with safety and prosperity. Remember the context of this passage is the threat of being conquered by Assyria.

Notice that proper living involves not only actions but also words. A person could be moral and upright but use words carelessly, speaking insults and put-downs, and expressing anger. The righteous person avoids seeing evil and listening to evil. In our own time, we could easily transpose the ancient text to apply to the modern media and the Internet; but generally, the text applies to any situation that the righteous person knows to avoid.

What are contemporary examples of "the gain of oppression"? Why do you think looking, listening, and speaking are so important in the Scripture reading and in contemporary life?

REFLECT

Bible Facts
The Israelites lived in two kingdoms, but the larger nations of the region posed a threat. The Northern Kngdom fell in 722 B.C. to the Assyrians, and the Southern Kingdom fell to the Babylonians in 586 B.C.

BIBLE FACTS

What Does God Require?
Micah 6:6-8

Micah preached from the mid 700's B.C. to about the 680's B.C. In Micah 6, we discover another expression of what God requires of God's people.

What's in the Bible?
Read Micah 6:6-8. What immediate insights do you gain as you read this Scripture? How does it clarify God's will for your life?

Micah 5:2–6:5 promises great things in the future for Israel and recalls the things God has done on behalf of the people. In one of our previous readings, Moses similarly recalled for the Israelites all the things God had done for them (Deuteronomy 6:10-12). Instead, the people seem "wearied" of God (Micah 6:3). This isn't an untypical response. God's blessings are many, but we are also liable to forget them. Serving God can be difficult, and sometimes we can become discouraged.

Verse 7 contains ideas about worship that are challenging and different from worship in our contemporary churches. While it is challenging to think about sacrifices and burnt offerings in our age, one question emerges that is timeless: Can you ever do enough for God? Would thousands of rams and millions of gallons of oil, and even your child, be enough for God? God forbade human sacrifices; but according to 2 Kings 16:3; 21:6; and Jeremiah 7:31, the practice persisted. The question in Micah 6:7 is rhetorical and sarcastic. Though important, worship isn't a procedure, program, or formula by which we "get right" with God. No, God has shown us what is required: "To do justice, and to love kindness, / and to walk humbly with your God" (verse 8).

Do Justice

In the Bible, the word that is translated "justice" has meanings related to the legal systems and to attributes of God and God's people. The word has also been translated as "righteousness." The concept of justice as an attribute of God indicates that God cares, especially for those who are vulnerable. Justice is an essential principle of life together as God's people. God is just, therefore, God's people are called to be just—and in Micah 6:8—to *do* justice.

Sometimes justice is clear-cut: People have been harmed or killed, and the perpetrators need to be punished and the victims vindicated. When we reflect on issues of social justice, we encounter gray areas and sincere differences of opinion. Name a social issue, and you're liable to find widely conflicting opinions. Little wonder that Christians so often focus on questions of individual morality. It is easier to follow the Ten Commandments than to erase poverty, to make petroleum cheaper, to decrease crime, or to ensure suitable wages and health care in companies. However, our efforts for justice begin with our own behavior, convictions, and attitudes.

What thoughts come to your mind when you hear the word justice? *How do you think individuals and communities can do justice?*

REFLECT

Love Kindness

Micah 6:8 says, "Love kindness." The word *kindness* can also be translated "mercy." It means much more than just being nice. It suggests active goodness and faithfulness and is a key feature of relationship with God and with one another. As with justice, kindness is frequently mentioned in the Bible as an attribute of God (Exodus 34:6). Again, God's people should love kindness because God loves kindness. Life can make us self-reliant, performance-oriented, and hardheaded. If we're not careful, our religious faith can be distorted with those qualities. Christians are called to be different and to express kindness, trust, generosity, and forgiveness. Paul understood kindness as a fruit of the Spirit (Galatians 5:24), and he zeroed in on kindness and gentleness as essential Christian traits (Ephesians 4:31-32; Philippians 4:5).

What thoughts come to mind when you hear the word kindness? *How do you think people can do kindness as well as love kindness?*

REFLECT

Walk Humbly With God

The third requirement in Micah 6:8 is to walk humbly with God. The word *humble* may also mean "to walk carefully or wisely."[1] The key idea is to walk with God and to place God first in one's life. We are called to a double humility: humility before the righteous God and humility in our dealings with others. Humble people do not have exalted opinions of themselves. Rather, they have an appreciation of who they are in relation to God and to other persons. Humility is not the same as humiliation. It is a positive attitude that allows people to learn, to grow, to appreciate, and to love.

What thoughts come to your mind when you hear the word humble*?*
How do you understand the idea of walking humbly with God?

R E F L E C T

Like an Ever-flowing Stream
Amos 5:21-24

Amos was a contemporary of Micah and Isaiah. Amos 5:21-24 is a wonderful complement to the Micah passage we read. A Bible scholar notes that "Amos does not intend to replace ritual with social action. Rather, what happens in society must correspond to what is said and done in worship. Amos tells us that God does not accept the worship of those who show no interest in justice in their daily lives."[2] As shown in other Bible passages, God hears the distress of the needy (Psalms 68:5-6; 140:12); and God calls us to hear as well (Proverbs 19:17; 21:13; 28:27). God doesn't ignore the poor and destitute or blame them for their plight, as we so often do. Rather, God takes their side and calls upon us to respond to them in God's name.

What's in the Bible?
Read Amos 5:21-24. What challenges you in this Scripture? How does it speak to you about God's love for justice?

?

The climax of this Scripture is Amos 5:24, which says, "But let justice roll down like waters, / and righteousness like an ever-flowing stream." Water is an excellent metaphor for justice. Water is necessary for life. Water cleanses and renews. It's also a strong force; it carries objects and cuts through rock and soil. In Amos's passage, water is also plentiful. An abundance of water in a dry region is as welcome as justice in a society ruled by injustice.

In the tradition of the prophets, Jesus offered good news to the poor (Luke 4:18). He calls us to be sensitive to their needs and to prove our worship by addressing people's needs, loneliness, and deprivation (Matthew 25:31-46).

Years ago, I was assisting with Communion at a downtown church. A man who was obviously intoxicated came forward. "Would you like Communion?" I asked as he knelt. "Yeah!" he said proudly. After the service, the pastor spent time talking to him. At the time, I felt intimidated by a drunk at the altar rail; but in retrospect, I realize God desires justice for people just like that man. Churches spend a lot of time figuring out how to market their programs to the community. Imagine, however, a church with several people who live on the streets, people who are struggling with alcohol or drugs, a few people on parole, and others of whom you disapprove. Would you welcome such people into your spotless church built for outreach? The prophets challenge us to reach out to them with justice and mercy.

Sometimes we don't integrate our Bible-based ideas and our political views, so we have hardhearted opinions that are contrary to Bible teachings. I've known sincere Christians whose political talk is angry, unloving, and dismissive of the poor. I have heard them say such things as "The poor are lazy, ungrateful, wasteful, and want to cheat honest taxpayers"; but imagine if God took a hardhearted attitude toward us. "[Your name] is just lazy and should've avoided that situation. I'll no longer respond to [you] with help and forgiveness." Imagine if God told you coldly, "Deal with it yourself! No more grace for you!"

Knowing how to help the needy is difficult. Supporting local assistance groups (through contributions and/or volunteer help) can be a good thing. Social justice advocates remind us that we not only need to give money to charities and missions but also to help support means by which the poor can be self-sufficient. As important as a church-supported soup kitchen is, a church could go a step further and support people who are interviewing for jobs, help people find housing, or help parolees move back into society.[3]

These aren't necessarily comfortable things to do, and not all of us have the savvy or ability to perform such ministries. So we need to pray for God's grace and wisdom in knowing how best to help others. Jesus' famous saying, "You always have the poor with you" (John 12:8) is less a comment on the perpetual nature of poverty as a challenge: We'll always have opportunities to help people.

How does your church provide help to the community? In what other ways do you think your church might respond to Amos's call to "let justice roll down like waters / and righteousness like an ever-flowing stream"?

REFLECT

New Covenant
Jeremiah 31:31-34

Starting fresh can be a good thing. My wife and I like to grow in our professions and find new challenges, which means that we have moved a few times. Change can be difficult, though. As I write this, we're getting ready to send our daughter off to college. Meanwhile, I'm helping my mother adjust to a nursing home. Pastors and laity commonly struggle to bring newness to a congregation. How do you help people catch fire for service? Many of us are already stretched thin in our lives, but God is always ready to help us start fresh.

The hymn "Great Is Thy Faithfulness" contains the line "Morning by morning, new mercies I see." While we fallible humans aren't likely to extend second and third chances indefinitely, God works with us each day of our lives, no matter what. Jeremiah 31:31-34 expresses God's renewing power in terms of a new covenant.

What's in the Bible?
Read Jeremiah 31:31-34. When have you started afresh, or started over, in your life? What are the plusses and minuses of starting again? What is the new situation that Jeremiah envisions?

Jeremiah was a prophet whose ministry coincided with the dark and terrible time up to and including the Babylonian siege and eventual destruction of Jerusalem in 588-586 B.C. Covenant is a strong theme throughout the Bible. Here, Jeremiah talks about the new covenant: "I will put my law within them, and I will write it on their hearts; and I will be their God, and they shall be my people (verse 33). In the New Testament, Jesus is the fulfillment of this prophecy (Hebrews 8:1-13). Now God extends his power and blessing to all people. All people who look to Christ seek to give themselves to God so God's will and law is an inner desire.

BIBLE FACTS

Bible Facts

Several passages in the prophets talk about newness. Ezekiel talks about a new spirit and a new heart (11:19-20; 36:26). To have a new heart means to become a new person. A related heart image is found in Deuteronomy 30:6, where Moses refers to the circumcision of the heart as a metaphor for obedience. Circumcision (performed on Jewish baby boys at age eight days) is a sign of the covenant, and a circumcision of the heart means that our emotions and intellect are so focused upon God that we ourselves become signs of the covenant.

Giving ourselves to God wholeheartedly isn't easy. Most of us surrender to God most readily when we're in trouble, and that's a great time to turn to God; but our human nature is such that we get along on our own strength and initiative when times are good. I can testify how wonderful it feels to give ourselves to God each day, including the good days; but we need time (perhaps years) to grow in faith so we're continually opening to God and experiencing God's loving Spirit. In returning to God, we discover that God empowers our life together as just and merciful people.

Here's Why I Care
God calls us to give our hearts to him; but once we do, we must allow God to train our hearts so that we're eager for justice, concerned for the needy, and motivated by kindness and compassion. How is your heart right now?

A Prayer

Lord, we need to know your will through our minds, emotions, and loyalties. Help us give ourselves to you more fully and to see one another as you see us; in Christ we pray. Amen.

---

[1]From *The New Interpreter's Bible* (Abingdon Press, 1996); page 581.
[2]From *The New Interpreter's Bible;* page 394.
[3]From *Standing in the Margin: How Your Congregation Can Minister With the Poor (and Perhaps Recover Its Soul in the Process)*, by Mary Alice Mulligan and Rufus Burrow, Jr. (The Pilgrim Press, 2004); page 123.

Chapter Three

Jesus Teaches
God's Way

Bible Readings
Matthew 18:21-35; Mark 7:1-23; Luke 6:17-49; John 13:1-20

The Questions
What does Jesus teach about God's way? How do these teachings tell us about life together as God's people? How can following the teachings of Jesus affect our life together?

_____

_____

_____

_____

_____

_____

_____

_____

_____

_____

_____

_____

_____

A Psalm

Praise the LORD!

How good it is to sing praises to our God;

for he is gracious, and a song of praise is fitting.

The LORD builds up Jerusalem;

he gathers the outcasts of Israel.

He heals the brokenhearted,

and binds up their wounds.

He determines the number of the stars;

he gives to all of them their names.

Great is our Lord, and abundant in power;

his understanding is beyond measure.

The LORD lifts up the downtrodden;

he casts the wicked to the ground.

Psalm 147:1-6

A Prayer

Lord, we know that the teachings of Jesus hold your vision for our life together; but we don't always know how best to follow them. Heal our wounds, and lift us up so we might be a people in your name. Amen.

Savior and Teacher

Jesus taught great things that anyone could follow, but we miss the crucial thing about Jesus if we make him only a terrific moral teacher. Jesus rescues us from the power of sin, offers salvation and healing, and gives us power for living. He helps us live a life according to God's will and vision for us. Through Jesus, God forgives us and helps us when we fail. Yet, through the teachings of Jesus, we learn about what it means to live as God's people. He usually taught groups of people: his circle of disciples, interested crowds, and opponents. Jesus' teachings were aimed at bringing people together and helping them live together as his followers.

What do you know about the teachings of Jesus? How do you understand God's work of salvation through Jesus Christ?

R E F L E C T

The King and Two Slaves
Matthew 18:21-35

Sometimes we attend church in an individualistic way. We like a church that meets our needs; and if something at church offends us, we go elsewhere. In Jesus' teachings, we all have a responsibility for one another. He is especially present when we're gathered with other Christians (Matthew 18:20). He commands Christians to make the effort to forgive and uphold one another (18:15-20). In this context, Peter poses a famous question: How much should we forgive (verse 21)?

What's in the Bible?
Read Matthew 18:21-35. What challenges you about Jesus' teaching in this Scripture? In your personal experience, what are the benefits and challenges associated with forgiveness?

Jesus' response as recorded in the Greek language of the New Testament could be translated either "77 times" or "7 times 70 times." Jesus may have been speaking humorously. When I was in grade school, we'd say "a googleplex times infinity" to indicate an outrageous number. Jesus' answer of 77, or 490, is meant the same way: You can't tabulate and quantify forgiveness. You just forgive, and you never stop forgiving!

Jesus' story vividly depicts forgiveness. The king insisted that his slave repay a debt; but the slave's debt was "ten thousand talents," which would be millions of dollars. The slave humbled himself; and, amazingly, the king forgave him the outrageously large debt. However, the slave went out, abused a fellow slave, and had him imprisoned for debt. The second slave owed him a hundred denarii—several months' worth of income but far short of the many years' worth of wages the first slave owed the king.

Usually when we receive a second chance in a terrible situation, we feel elated and want to do better. Not so, this man. On hearing the news, the king reneged on his forgiveness and dealt cruelly with the first slave. This could be a simple story of forgiveness: How awful is an unforgiving spirit—the first slave's and the king's. The story may also be interpreted as an allegory wherein God is the king and the different debts represent sin. It calls us to be merciful and forgiving of one another as God is merciful and forgiving of us.

Once again, we are called to express an attribute of God in our life together. We are called to forgive as God forgives.

Bible Facts

Slavery is an institution mentioned in the Bible; but rather than encouraging it, the Torah contains laws that addressed the problem of indebtedness, which in turn was a way to slavery in the ancient world. Leviticus 25:8-55 and Deuteronomy 15:1-18 concern the release of debts and the provision for the freedom of slaves. Although slavery existed in the Middle Eastern kingdoms and the Roman Empire, God's laws provided opportunities for relief and release, ensuring a benevolent life together among rich and poor.[1]

BIBLE FACTS

Aspects of Forgiveness

Let's think together, in a general way, about aspects of forgiveness. We can forgive people of their crimes, but shouldn't they suffer the consequences of their actions? We could forgive a person, but will forgiveness rebuild the relationship? Forgiveness changes us for the better but doesn't necessarily change the other person. Our forgiveness might help that person, or he or she might remain as hurtful and unapologetic as ever.

We must use common sense and understanding in gauging the situation and the character of the other person. We also need to be self-aware so we don't use forgiveness in a self-punishing or passive-aggressive way. A false, manipulative forgiveness can be destructive; but a true, Spirit-given forgiveness can be a crucial step in healing. Sometimes, we are the ones who must be forgiven. If we are the recipient of another's forgiveness, we have been given a great gift if we choose to accept that forgiveness; or we may have done something and find it difficult to forgive ourselves.

Bitterness is a way of retaining power over the person who hurt us. Here's the "reasoning": If I stay angry at that person, I keep him or her diminished. That person is bad because he or she hurt me; and as long as I stay angry, that person will always be bad and "small." Who is hurt by our anger? Probably not the person who hurt us, who possibly doesn't even know how we feel. Holding on to our bitterness gives the one who has wronged us power over us, power to hurt us months and years after the original incident.

We gain strength and freedom when we forgive. We find strength to keep moving in our lives. The person who once had power to hurt us can do so no longer (or at least not in a way that holds us captive). When we forgive, we are able to refocus our emotional energies; and we are able to grow closer to God. Christ has already removed the divisions between us (Ephesians 2:14-17), and so forgiveness actualizes a condition that already exists. When we grow in forgiveness, we begin to understand the heart of God.

Like love, forgiveness isn't the result of heroic willpower. It is a gift of God. We might have to admit that we find forgiveness impossible; the other person just hurt us too badly. God already knows our feelings and still loves us. God can work healing power in our lives when we admit to God our deep feelings of hatred, hurt, and anger. This, too, has biblical precedent, for the psalmists were quite forthright in their prayers.

Forgiveness is a powerful sign of our life together, not only in specific instances of forgiveness but also in Christian fellowship. If love and trust are present in our fellowship, we can discuss our painful feelings with one another.

How difficult is it for you to forgive someone who has hurt you? How difficult is it to accept forgiveness? Which seems most diffi-cult—to forgive or to be forgiven? Why? In your relationships with others, have you ever experienced that forgiveness that came as a gift from God rather than the result of your own efforts? What was it like? When it is hard to forgive or to be forgiven, how do you think the power of God can help?

REFLECT

From the Heart
Mark 7:1-23

In the ancient traditions of worship, certain things were deemed holy and unclean (not holy); and as such, they held a kind of power. Holy things had to be approached in a certain way because people could be killed by the power of holiness (Leviticus 10:1-3; 2 Samuel 6:6-7). Unclean things were risky, too, and conferred a negative power from which one needed to be cleansed (Leviticus 11–15). When Isaiah called himself a "man of unclean lips," he acknowledged that his own speech didn't have the holiness power of God's own words (Isaiah 6:1-8). In Jesus' lifetime, people sometimes told him to go away because they perceived a holiness power in him that might be dangerous (Matthew 8:34).

What's in the Bible?
Read Mark 7:1-23. What insights does this Scripture offer you about life together as God's people? How do you respond to the association between holiness and cleanliness? How does this Scripture speak to contemporary life?

The concern for holiness lies behind the traditions associated with purity that were practiced during Jesus' time. Jesus himself was an observant Jew. After he healed a leper, he instructed him to undergo rites of purity (Mark 1:41-44). Then Jesus encouraged the Jewish disciples in fasting, in reconciliation among worshipers, and in prayer (Matthew 6:1-18). Rather than being hostile to Jewish practices, Jesus harkened back to a concern of the Hebrew prophets: Formal worship requires inner purity, or it is meaningless (Mark 7:6-7).

Jesus also discussed a rabbinical concern of the time. The Corban law concerned those persons who vowed to give items or money to God by giving it to the Temple. What if such a vow interfered with one's responsibilities to one's parents? This was a case where one was "making void the word of God" by using a religious practice to avoid a commandment.

Love and holiness are essential to true worship. Food goes into us, and whatever is undigested comes back out. However, our hearts are the true source of uncleanness. From our hearts' uncleanness come the waste products that are evil words, deeds, and attitudes that hurt others.

R
E
F
L
E
C
T

Many of us are familiar with the term Freudian slip. *Can you think of times when you said something you didn't mean to say? Have you ever been embarrassed that your private words were unintentionally overheard? What was the situation? What connections do you see between such situations and what Jesus teaches in Mark 7:1-23?*

Sermon on the Plain
Luke 6:17-49

Luke 6:17-49 is Luke's version of the Sermon on the Mount (Matthew 5–7). Luke placed the teaching not on a mountain but on a plain (Luke 6:17), and the audience includes the disciples rather than a crowd (verse 20). Luke's version is also shorter than Matthew's three-chapter version.

What's in the Bible?
Read Luke 6:17-49. What challenges you in this Scripture? What insights does it offer you about life together?

Rich and Poor

If you feel disdain for poor people, avoid Luke's Gospel. One of Luke's themes is the blessedness of the poor, not just "the poor in spirit" (Matthew 5:3). The gospel is good news preached to the poor (Luke 1:52-53; 4:1-19). As we saw in our study of Amos and Micah, God has special love for the poor. When the kingdom of God comes, the poor will be redeemed, given pride and joy. The hungry will have food; the sorrowful will find happiness.

What about the rich? According to Jesus, the tables will turn on them in the Kingdom if wealth is at the center of their lives and concern for the poor is lacking. Not all concern about money is selfish, but love of money always carries a spiritual risk. A lack of money is a terrible source of heartache and worry, and unfortunately the emotional scars of indebtedness can hurt a person's faith in God's care. It's tough to hang on to God's promises when you're choosing between paying for your medicine and buying food or when you made a financial decision that seemed sensible but now is failing. An abundance of money is a source of heartache, too, because in times of prosperity, we still worry about money. Somehow we never feel as if we have enough.

We have to examine our hearts. Ask yourself: What is the state of my finances? How worried am I about having a bigger house or a bigger vehicle than my neighbor? With each salary promotion, do I think, "If only I had just a little more money"? The question that resonates beneath such concerns is the question about what means most in one's life. Who or what do we worship, and how does it affect our life together?

Read again Luke 6:20-25. How do you respond to the teachings about the rich and the poor? How do concerns about wealth and poverty relate to life together?

REFLECT

Love and Judgment

Jesus teaches us to love our enemies and to do good things for those who dislike or hate us. Essentially Jesus challenges us to be different, that is, to love like God. God is merciful and kind even to the wicked and ungrateful. Anyone can love his or her friends. Churches are full of people who are friends, but how do you treat someone well who has hurt you? How do you give without expectation of return? That's love as God loves.

In a similar vein, Jesus tells us not to judge others but to first examine ourselves and deal with our faults. Our human nature leads us otherwise. Many of us accept our faults while being critical of others. We feel good about denigrating others. We talk about people behind their backs. We speak harsh words and expect the person just to "take it." The Bible instructs us to correct one another when necessary but in a spirit of gentleness (Galatians 6:1). Criticism is not a fruit of the Spirit (Galatians 5:22-24).

Jesus cautions us about the attitudes of our hearts. It's one thing to say, "That person stole money from the treasury and needs to be appropriately punished." It's another to say, "That person stole money and ought to be strung up by his thumbs and horsewhipped." People who hurt us and arouse our moral outrage are, unfortunately, not lovable.

Jesus teaches that "no good tree bears bad fruit" and "the good person out of the good treasure of the heart produces good . . . for it is out of the abundance of the heart that the mouth speaks" (Luke 6:43-45). If we want a good gauge for our spiritual health, we need to listen to the things we say, not only to other people but also in private about other people. Our words reflect our relationship with God as well as with others.

Read again Luke 6:26-45. Which teachings are most challenging? most appealing? Why? How do they speak to you about life together?

REFLECT

Serving Others
John 13:1-17

Several years ago, my pastor preached on John 13:1-20. He announced that he would have footwashing during the service and that he'd give women time to leave the sanctuary to remove their hose while others could remove their shoes and socks. After the worshipers shifted uncomfortably in the pews for a couple seconds, the pastor said he was just kidding! Later, when he did preach on the John text, the pastor noted the difficulties many of us would have carrying out Jesus' instructions literally.

What's in the Bible?
Read John 13:1-17. How do you respond to this account of foot-washing? What appeals to you in this Scripture? What challenges you? How does it speak to life together?

In this narrative, Jesus sets an example for his disciples to follow. Verse 1 alerts us that Jesus is performing this act because he loved these disciples, though they didn't love him as faithfully in return (shown by Judas's betrayal, Peter's denial, and the absence of most of them when Jesus suffered).

Footwashing was a sign of hospitality in the ancient world. The host provided water and cloth, and then the guests washed themselves or allowed a servant to wash them. Today, we show love and hospitality in other ways, although women tell me that pedicures are wonderful and relaxing.

Jesus' key point is serving one another out of love. He loved the disciples, though they didn't yet grasp the depth of his love. He called them to deeper levels of love and service: "So if I, your Lord and Teacher, have washed your feet, you also ought to wash one another's feet" (John 13:14). Jesus calls us to love him so much that we put ourselves completely in his care and to love others so much that we're willing to serve one another with humility and complete love.

What contemporary examples of hospitality would demonstrate our commitment to love and service?

REFLECT

Love and Life Together

In all of these teachings, Jesus pointed out what is necessary for life together according to God's vision and God's way. At the heart of all his teachings is the call to love God and neighbor and to demonstrate our love through serving God and neighbor.

Here's Why I Care

Jesus gives us amazing grace and calls us to amazing love. Which of the teachings of Jesus covered in this session meant most to you? Why? What can you do this week to live out this teaching?

A Prayer

God, you call us to relationships and service beyond the expectations of the everyday world. Help us be ready for opportunities to express your love according to the teachings of Jesus; in Christ we pray. Amen.

---

[1]From *God and His Image: An Outline of Biblical Theology*, by Dominique Barthélemy (Ignatius, 2007); pages 85-90.

Chapter Four

Jesus Invites Us
Into God's Kingdom

Bible Readings
Luke 8:1-18; 10:1-24; 12:22-32; 13:8-21; 14:15-24; 17:20-21; and 18:16-24

The Questions
What is the kingdom of God? How do we recognize it? What does it mean to live in God's kingdom?

A Psalm

All your works shall give thanks to you, O LORD,
>and all your faithful shall bless you.

They shall speak of the glory of your kingdom,
>and tell of your power,

to make known to all people your mighty deeds,
>and the glorious splendor of your kingdom.

Your kingdom is an everlasting kingdom,
>and your dominion endures throughout all generations.

>Psalm 145:10-13

A Prayer

Lord, we want our hearts to be ready for your grace. Prevent us from missing your kingdom because we misunderstood it or were too worried and busy to see; in Christ's name. Amen.

God's Kingdom and Life Together

Jesus often taught in parables, small, easy-to-remember stories or situations that teach a larger point. Our last Bible readings are parables that teach us about God's kingdom, which is referred to in the Gospels as the kingdom of heaven or the kingdom of God.

What is God's kingdom? A key theme in Jesus' teachings, the kingdom of God signifies a specific kind of life for humans and for all creation now and in the future. It refers to the hope of God's reign at the end of all time and to living according to God's will today. Those who seek to live in the Kingdom are those who seek to do God's will in the world. When we talk about God's kingdom, we are not just talking about our individual salvation. We are also describing our life together as we grow in God's likeness and will. It means living as individuals and as communities in the power, will, and rule of God. Jesus' parables about the kingdom offer great insight about our life together as God's people.

Parable of the Sower
Luke 8:1-18

Our first Scripture is the parable of the sower. In this parable, Jesus tells us about spiritual "green thumbs" and "plant killers."

What's in the Bible?
Read Luke 8:1-18. What images especially appeal to you? Why? What does it say to you about life together in God's power and rule?

In Jesus' time, agricultural images were familiar to most people. This parable is true to life for those who first heard it. The seed is God's word, and many people accept that word in their hearts; but not all hearts are good environments for God's word. In some cases, a person's heart is like a path that is worn and has become hard. The seed can't take root and is brushed away by footsteps or eaten by birds. In some cases, the seed takes root among rocks and grows for a while; but plants usually can't grow like that because they can't take lasting root in the scarce soil among rocks. Jesus says that the rocks represent times of testing. Difficult circumstances can threaten a newly sown faith.

Have you ever attended a spiritual retreat or a revival? A person attending such an event feels excited about Jesus and even makes important life changes; but after the event concludes, when he or she goes back to the hard work of applying faith to everyday, non-religious circumstances, keeping faith may be difficult. The experience of a spiritual high is often followed by times of discouragement. The seed God has planted seems to have withered away.

What kind of soil have you been in your life? How would you describe the plant of your faith right now: dropping leaves, dried up, about to bloom, or growing great and putting out shoots?

REFLECT

Jesus also says that thorns, that is, cares and riches and pleasures, can prevent long-term spiritual growth. Problems can make a person disillusioned. When I was younger, I had the foolish notion that Christians shouldn't have any problems—a common misconception among Christians. Happiness and money can distract us from God, too. If life is going well, we don't turn to God as frequently as when we're in distress. Churches are filled with "rugged individualists" who know they can handle life, but we need a faith that seeks God's help through good times and bad.

What thorns crowd, choke, or smother your growth in faith?

REFLECT

Luke 8:16-17 inspired me tremendously when I first came seriously to the Christian message. I had modest musical and artistic talent, and I loved to lead people and to write. I wanted to discover ways I could use my talents for God.

The parable reminds us that while our intentions can be good, we can also experience challenges to the growth of our faith. Even though salvation is free, growth in love takes time and work. It helps to remember, however, that the main work of growth is empowered by God. God offers what we need in order to grow, and we also work with God's help to grow in God's love. Just as a marriage or a friendship will wither if we don't attend to the relationship, so our life of faith withers if we neglect to seek God's help through devotion, prayer, and service to God and others.

What talents or skills can you offer God and others? How do you think doing so would affect life together in God's kingdom?

REFLECT

No Shoes, No Cash, No Problem
Luke 10:1-24

Why must faith take root in our hearts and minds? Not only for our own sakes but also for the benefit of others. In our next story, Jesus sends out disciples to visits places he intended to visit. The disciples went out in pairs, visiting homes, curing people of their diseases, and telling them about the kingdom of God.

Read Luke 10:1-24. What's your comfort level in sharing your faith?

(1) I like to share my faith with people.

(2) My faith is too personal, and I'm too shy.

(3) I'd like to share my faith, but I'm not sure how.

(4) What faith?

This text alerts us to the importance of reaching out to others with the hope of life and healing in God's kingdom. This text also alerts us to the importance of interpreting the Bible so it can be understood in our contemporary context. If you take the Bible literally, then Jesus is sending all of us out, on foot with no money or provisions, with instructions to invite ourselves into people's homes. What might have worked well in the culture of Jesus' day is not likely to fare as well in our culture, but the question remains: How do we offer the hope of life together in God's kingdom? What does this text teach us?

I have worked on church programs for welcoming visitors. At one church, my friends and I made sure that volunteers were in place to call on visitors on Sunday afternoon. We checked records and hurried to find fill-ins if the scheduled volunteers didn't show up, because if volunteers didn't show up, we felt that we had missed the opportunity for a quick contact. I have to admit that many Sundays, I wondered if there was a better way. How can a congregation help members become excited about reaching out with love and care to newcomers, to people who may or may not welcome us?

Luke 10:1-24 does not guarantee success or ease as we reach out; but in the Bible reading, Jesus' instructions to the disciples are clear. Being called to enter the life and wholeness of God's kingdom means being called to offer the invitation to others in order that God's kingdom will grow. Followers of Jesus speak and live on behalf of Jesus Christ. "Whoever listens to you listens to me, and whoever rejects you rejects me, and whoever rejects me rejects the one who sent me" (Luke 10:16). As followers of Jesus, we share in the life of God; and we are empowered by God through Jesus Christ. Through our words and actions, those who hear and see us may enter life together in God's kingdom.

Who has been important to you as an example or teacher of God's way of life in Christ? Why?

REFLECT

Parables of the Kingdom
Luke 12:22-32; 13:18-21; 14:15-24

Many of the stories or parables of Jesus deal with particular aspects of life in God's kingdom. We will look at several in Luke's Gospel.

Do Not Worry
Luke 12:22-32

Luke 12:22-32 is a good passage for anyone who struggles with anxiety.

What's in the Bible?
Read Luke 12:22-32. What challenges you in this Scripture? Why?
How does it speak to you about God's kingdom?

Would you call yourself a calm person, a worrier about some things, or a worrier about most things? (I'm the second one.) If you grew up in a tense household or had some kind of trauma, you may be more geared toward anxiety than others; thus your anxiety is difficult to turn off and on. Yet God calls us to have no anxieties about anything as we give God our cares and concerns.

I don't want to make a simplistic equation: Seek God, and all else in life will be well. Sometimes we're seeking God, and life is totally insane and crazy. My own experience is that God is faithful over the long haul. I have certainly had stressful times, some of which lasted for years. As I've sought to do God's will in a variety of circumstances, God has never failed me.

God is intimately involved for good in every moment of our lives, whether we realize it or not. Emotions come and go, and troubles come and go; but God's love is constant. It does not grow warm and cold based on our feelings and behavior. We can trust God's love in all of life's circumstances.

How do you think God can help you grow in calmness and trust?
How do you think a person can overcome anxiety? List strategies.

REFLECT

52

Small Things Count
Luke 13:18-21

Luke 13:18-21 offers the hope of growth to all who may feel that what they have to offer to life together in God's kingdom is small or insignificant.

What's in the Bible?
Read Luke 13:18-21. Which image speaks most to you? Why? What does it say to you about life together in God's kingdom?

Mustard seeds are tiny, but they grow into sizable plants that nurture birds. Yeast is microscopic fungi, so it's even smaller; but yeast is potent for leavening. In Jesus' story, the yeast leavened that whole batch of flour. Jesus says the Kingdom is like that: a tremendous result from tiny beginnings.

These verses have inspired me in my own efforts to live faithfully. It's so easy for us to slip into a performance-oriented way of thinking: I'm not a good Christian unless I do this, this, and this. Life, after all, requires that we advance ourselves through our accomplishments, education, recommendations, and appearance. What we do or what we have to offer may seem small or insignificant. We don't always know the outcome of our actions.

One small, personal example is my childhood vacation Bible school. I suppose the pastor at the time reported the numbers of enrolled children in his year's end reports to denominational officials; but did the pastor report, "One of our little boys will get so excited about faith after he grows up that years from now he'll write Sunday school study books"? Of course not! God's work in my life had been planted but was not yet evident. God's work happens in amazing ways that can't always be observed, measured, and reported.

What small actions have you seen that yielded large, positive results?
What connections do you see to Jesus' parables of growth?

REFLECT

God's Invitation
Luke 14:15-24

A friend once complained, half jokingly, that the only way you get a thank-you note for a wedding gift these days is to include a self-addressed stamped envelope with the gift. Sometimes people have a lax approach to accepting social invitations, too. This Scripture reminds us that people have always been a little careless about gestures of sociality and hospitality.

What's in the Bible?
Read Luke 14:15-24. What challenges you in this Scripture? Why?
What connections do you make between this Scripture and life together in God's kingdom?

In this story, the person throwing a party must have been well to-do; but those who were invited chose not to come to the great party. Everyone gave excuses, from the important to the shallow. Angry, the host told his slaves to invite "the poor, the crippled, the blind, and the lame," and anyone else who would come.

The poor and disabled were neglected by society in Jesus' day; and, unfortunately, they are often neglected in our day. Jesus told this story of an invitation to a banquet when he was in the home of a leader of the Pharisees. In so doing, he challenged them to consider who God invites to God's table. God invites those who we may not consider desirable.

I think of our contemporary time. Lots of people are churchgoing Christians. That's a great thing to be, but how deeply do we follow him? Do we go through the motions of worship but don't respond to ways he calls us? As we saw in our previous sessions, we must be sure that our worship inspires in us a deep love of God which, in turn, grows into a deep love for other people, even those who may be different from us or those we may consider to be undesirable.

Think of ways God invites people to "eat bread in the kingdom of God." Do you think God ever feels disappointment? Why?

REFLECT

Inside and Outside
Luke 17:20-21; 18:16-24

The readings in Luke 17 and 18 also speak to our response to the invitation to life together in God's kingdom.

55

What's in the Bible?
Read Luke 17:20-21. What challenges you in this Scripture? Why?
What connections do you make between this Scripture and life
together in God's kingdom?

Our first reading is a short saying of Jesus: "The kingdom of God is not coming with things that can be observed; nor will they say, 'Look, here it is!' or 'There it is!' For, in fact, the kingdom of God is among you." The Greek preposition *entos*, used in the original language of this sentence, could mean "among" or "within." This ambiguity alerts us to the dual nature of God's kingdom. On one hand, God's power manifests itself in our inner being.

Remember Deuteronomy 6, which enlists us to love the Lord with our whole selves. However, growing in faith is a process. We learn to trust God more fully. We have good and bad experiences in our lives; and we see, often in hindsight, how God worked in our lives. Like the physical growth of children, we can't point to a child and say, "I see you growing," because the process is imperceptible. God's kingdom, however, isn't solitary, as we've already seen. When we're baptized, we are with others who are supporting us. When we take Communion, we do so together. When we feel God's love, we want to share it with others. When we grow in faith, we do so with other people. The kingdom of God is within us and among us.

In Luke 18:16-27, we find Jesus welcoming children and talking to the rich young ruler. In the first part of this passage, Jesus welcomes the little children who were brought to him. The disciples disapproved. Perhaps they wanted to protect Jesus' time, or perhaps they thought children were beneath Jesus' dignity; but Jesus replied that the kingdom of God belongs to "such as these." In fact, "whoever does not receive the kingdom of God as a little child will never enter it." What if Jesus had said, "Whoever does not receive the kingdom as an adult"? Then we'd assume that faith is self-reliant, perhaps a little jaded, and aggressive. However, children are trusting, eager, and excited about discovery. Can we describe our faith as childlike?

Think of qualities of children. Which qualities are good descriptions of religious faith? How do we, who are not children, grow in childlike faith?

REFLECT

57

The story of the rich ruler follows the story of the children. Perhaps we are meant to contrast the wholehearted sincerity of children with the more reserved response of the ruler. The story of the rich ruler is difficult and poignant. He had kept the Law, but apparently something was missing. Jesus saw into his heart. In keeping with an ongoing theme in Luke's Gospel, Jesus urged the relinquishment of possessions (Luke 12:33) and invited the ruler to follow him. The ruler was saddened by Jesus' response. The invitation was too hard.

Is this Scripture just about possessions? If I say, "Jesus is telling us to put him above our possessions and savings," that would take some of the seriousness out of Jesus' command. After all, Jesus could've told him exactly that: "Put me first in your priorities, above your possessions."

If I say, "Jesus is telling all of us to give away all that we have and live utterly in his care," we're faced with an impractical command that most of us could not follow. Jesus' invitation is to a specific man. Jesus saw that following the Law was not enough for the ruler. He offered him an opportunity for a richer life, an opportunity to follow him as a disciple. Jesus met the ruler where he was and offered him what he needed. The great tragedy of the story is that the ruler could not see beyond his wealth to a richer life in God's kingdom.

When have you had a sense of something more when things were apparently going well in your life? What was it like? What connections do you make between this experience in your life and the story of the rich ruler?

REFLECT

Eagerness and Reluctance

When confronted with the various qualities or characteristics of life together in God's kingdom, we all may experience eagerness and reluctance to let the seed grow, to let the bread be leavened, or to go to the dinner party. A ray of hope shines in the story of the rich ruler. When Jesus acknowledged how difficult it is for those who have wealth to enter God's kingdom, he also said, "What is impossible for mortals is possible for God." We are never alone in our seeking. We are never alone as we strive for life together according to God's will and rule.

Here's Why I Care
What Scriptures have meant most to you in this study about life together? Why? What is your present understanding of the kingdom? What steps can you take this week to participate in life together according to God's will and rule?

A Prayer

Lord, give us a faith that looks to you without reservations and with great love. Give us grace to see ways to serve one another; in Christ we pray. Amen.

APPENDIX
PRAYING THE BIBLE

Praying the Bible is an ancient process for engaging the Scriptures in order to hear the voice of God. It is also called *lectio divina*, which means "sacred reading." You may wish to use this process in order to become more deeply engaged with the Bible readings offered in each chapter of this study book. Find a quiet place where you will not be interrupted, a place where you can prayerfully read your Bible. Choose a Bible reading from a chapter in this study book. Use the following process to "pray" the Bible reading. After you pray the Bible reading, you may wish to record your experience in writing or through another creative response using art or music.

Be Silent
Open your Bible, and locate the Bible reading you have chosen. After you have found the reading, be still and silently offer all your thoughts, feelings, and hopes to God. Let go of concerns, worries, or agendas. Just *be* for a few minutes.

Read
Read the Bible reading slowly and carefully aloud or silently. Reread it. Be alert to any word, phrase, or image that invites you, intrigues you, confuses you, or makes you want to know more. Wait for this word, phrase, or image to come to you; and try not to rush it.

Reflect
Repeat the word, phrase, or image from the Bible reading to yourself and ruminate over it. Allow this word, phrase, or image to engage your thoughts, feelings, hopes, or memories.

Pray

Pray that God will speak to you through the word, phrase, or image from the Bible reading. Consider how this word, phrase, or image connects with your life and how God is made known to you in it. Listen for God's invitation to you in the Bible reading.

Rest and Listen

Rest silently in the presence of God. Empty your mind. Let your thoughts and feelings move beyond words, phrases, or images. Again, just *be* for a few minutes. Close your time of silent prayer with "Amen," or you may wish to end your silence with a spoken prayer.